Healthy Habits

Lemur's
Guide to
Healthy
Eating

Franklin Watts
First published in Great Britain in 2022 by The Watts Publishing Group

Credits
Commissioning editor: Sarah Peutrill
Series editor: Lisa Edwards
Series Designer: Rachel Lawston

HB ISBN: 978 1 4451 8232 2
PB ISBN: 978 1 4451 8238 4

Printed in China

FSC
MIX
Paper from
responsible sources
FSC® C104740

Franklin Watts
An imprint of
Hachette Children's Group
Part of Hodder & Stoughton
Carmelite House
50 Victoria Embankment
London EC4Y 0DZ

An Hachette UK Company
www.hachette.co.uk

www.hachettechildrens.co.uk

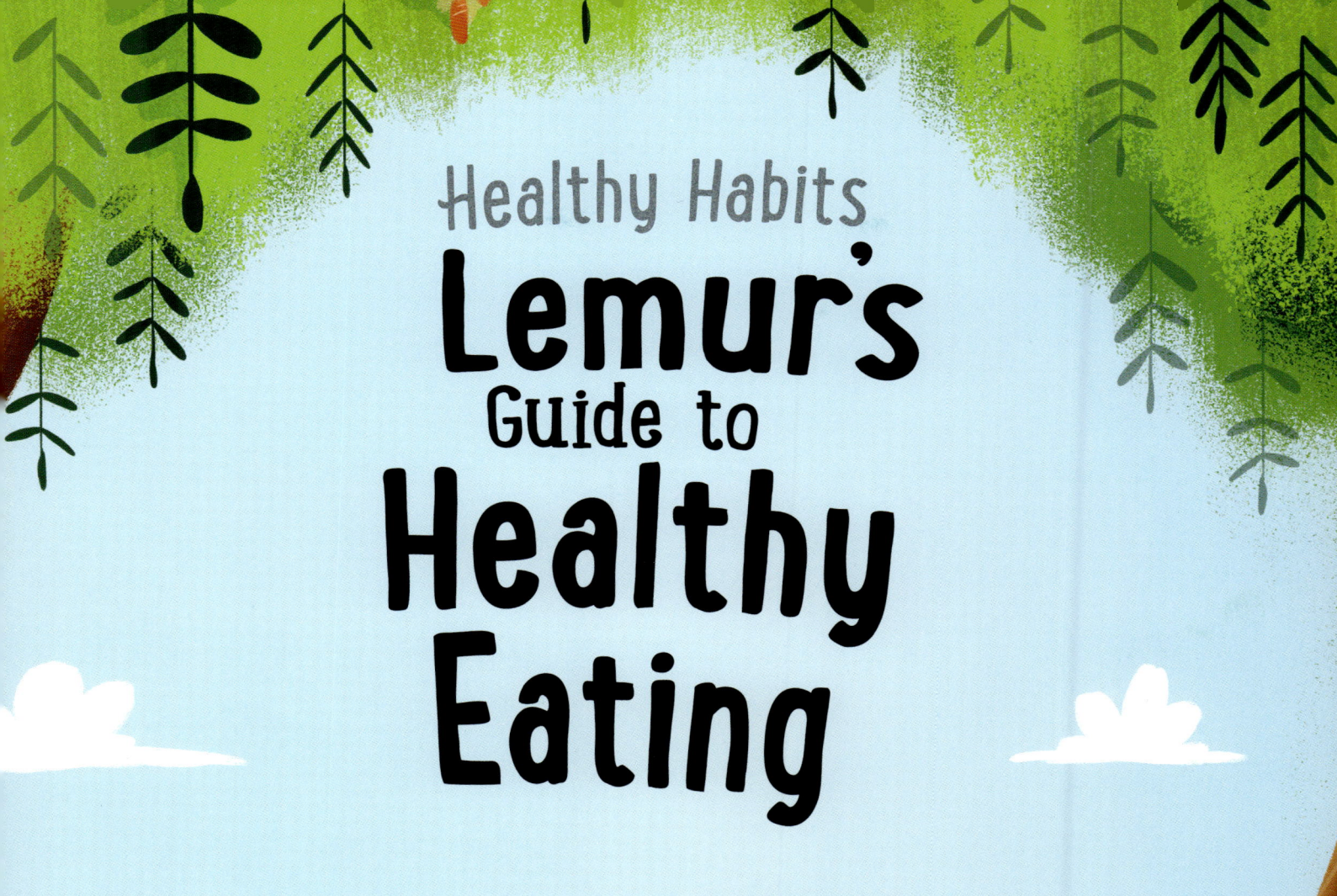

Healthy Habits

Lemur's Guide to Healthy Eating

Lisa Edwards   Siân Roberts

W

FRANKLIN WATTS
LONDON • SYDNEY

Lemur lives in a group called a troop.
The troop likes to eat together.

Chomp! Chomp!

poooooooof!

Crunch! Crunch!

It's good to sit down for meals with people you love and share your food.

Lemur loves eating the leaves of the tamarind tree in the morning.

6

Eating fresh, healthy food in the mornings
gives you enough energy to run and climb like Lemur!

Some porridge, or brown-bread toast with
a banana will give you all the energy you need.

Lemur finds lots of food on the forest floor.
Flowers, seeds and fruit fall from the trees above him.

Lemur makes sure he eats food that is fresh.

When it's fresh it has the most goodness still inside it.

Lemur eats lots of different foods to stay healthy, from plants to small insects.

He even eats wood and soil!

It's good to have a balanced diet containing lots
of different foods so your body gets everything it needs.
But wood and soil are for lemur, not you!

Lemur has to eat whatever he can find, whenever he can.
During the dry season in the forest, he mostly eats lettuce.

We can plan our meals to make sure we get everything we need every day – at least five portions of fruit and vegetables, filled with goodness.

Lemur is mostly vegetarian – he likes to eat plants. But sometimes, he likes to eat foods that contain protein, such as insects.

You need protein too, to make your body strong.
You can get it from meat and fish, but you can also
find it in eggs, milk, seeds, nuts and beans.

Lemur loves fruit that is full of fibre,
like bananas or figs.

Fibre makes the inside of his
body work properly.

You eat fibre when you have your favourite
cereal for breakfast or a piece of fruit.
It's also in vegetables such as broccoli.

Lemur drinks water from a stream
or licks leaves after it's been raining.

It's important for him to drink lots
of water, especially as it's hot where he lives.

Most of your body is made up of water so you need to drink six
to eight glasses a day. You can drink juice with your meals too.

Lemur loves tamarind tree pods as a healthy snack. He cracks the hard shell with his teeth and licks the sweet fruit inside.

You can snack on fruit like an apple or a peach, between your meals. Nuts and carrot sticks taste good too.

Lemur gets his energy to move around the forest mainly from fruit, which contains carbohydrates.

Putting carbohydrates into our bodies is like putting fuel into a car. The car doesn't move without it!

You get lots of energy from eating carbohydrate in foods such as vegetables, potatoes, brown bread, brown rice and cereal.

Lemur loves to play-fight with his friends and family.

He can play for a long time, without feeling tired.

This is because Lemur doesn't eat sugary foods like white bread, sweet cereal and chocolate bars.

Eating lots of sugary foods isn't good for you either. They can make you feel tired and harm your teeth.

Lemur makes the most of his forest home by eating a little of everything. His troop only takes what it needs – the rest is left for other creatures to share.

Why not try eating only as much as you need? If you're not too full, your body is free to do lots of other things!

Lemur has been showing us his healthy eating habits.

How can you eat more healthily?

Eat together and share what you have

Eat breakfast

Eat fresh food

Eat a varied and balanced diet

Make sure you eat fruit and vegetables

Eat protein

Eat fibre

Drink lots of water

Eat healthy snacks between meals

Eat carbohydrate

Avoid sugary foods

Eat what you need and no more

Glossary

Balanced diet when the food you eat every day is made up of fruit, vegetables, protein, carbohydrates and fibre.

Carbohydrates foods that give us lots of energy, coming from plants and milk

Energy the strength and power your body needs to move around

Fibre a type of carbohydrate in plants that passes through your body and keeps it healthy

Fuel something which is burned to produce heat or power

Protein found in animal and plant-based foods, protein makes our bodies grow strong

Vegetarian a person or animal that only eats plants

Let's talk about healthy habits...

The *Healthy Habits* series has been been written to help young children begin to understand how they can live healthy lives, both in their relationships with others and in their own bodies.

It provides a starting point for parents, carers and teachers to discuss healthy ways of being in the world with little learners. The series involves a cast of animal characters who behave in healthy ways in their own habitats, relating their experiences to familiar, everyday scenarios for children.

Lemur's Guide to Healthy Eating

This story looks at all the ways you can make sure you are eating a healthy, balanced diet.

The book aims to encourage a child's awareness of the food they are putting inside their bodies, and the importance of basic food groups. It offers children a simple checklist of items they need to eat and drink to maintain their health.

How to use the book:

The book is designed for adults to share with either an individual child, or a group of children, and as a starting point for discussion.

Choose a time when and the children are relaxed and have time to share the story.

Before reading the story:

- Spend time looking at the illustrations and talking about what the book might be about before reading it together. Ask the children to look at the details in each picture to see what all the creatures are doing – some of them are echoing the main themes in the background of the story.

- Encourage children to employ a 'phonics-first' approach to tackling new words by sounding them out.

After reading the story:

- Talk about the story with the children. Ask them what their favourite foods are. How does eating certain foods make them feel?

- Ask the children why they think it is important to eat healthily. How do they feel when they eat too much, especially sugary foods? Do they feel full of energy or tired?

- Place the children into four groups – one for breakfast, lunch, dinner and snacktime. Ask them to write out and draw a colourful menu of healthy things they would eat and drink at each meal.

- At the end of the session, discuss each meal plan with the whole class. Identify the major food groups – fruit and vegetables, protein, carbohydrates, fats and sugars.